# Healing Thoughts

### Reflections
by

Father Leo Booth

SCP LIMITED
2700 St. Louis Avenue
Long Beach, CA 90806


ISBN 0-9623282-1-9

© COPYRIGHT 1998
Leo Booth

This book is dedicated
to the
life and spirit
of
Princess Diana

# Contents

# LONELINESS

Sometimes I feel so lonely.

I feel that I am the only person
in this world.

Then I look at the stars and I
know that I am not alone.

I belong in this world.

Today is not a good day.
The news is depressing.

Friends seem absent…
I am alone.

But I am alive.

I have the precious gift
of freedom.

The choice to smile is
still mine.

Things are not going well
in my life.

I feel anxious.

I'm wallowing in depression.

Allowing myself to feel and
express this pain affirms a
healthier tomorrow.

The house is silent.

The telephone does not ring.

I need to walk out into
my world.

I need to say hello to
my neighbor.

The telephone works
both ways.

Today I feel restless.

Uncomfortable with my life.

Uncomfortable with my
feelings.

Uncomfortable
with my accomplishments.

Then I remember:
We are restless til we rest
in God.

Nobody cares!

I am alone.

A victim of life …
or so it seems.

Then a bird sings
in a tree.

I am
not alone.

God created the light
that casts a shadow.

Today I seem to be living
in that shadow.

Tomorrow I'll find
the light.

All I want to do is sleep.

Sleep in the pain of
my aching loneliness.

Why do I feel so lonely?

To be lonely is
to be human.

Today I understand —
it is okay to be lonely.

Friends surround me
and yet I feel alone.

Loneliness
stalks me in life.

Then I begin to tell somebody
that I am lonely, and the
loneliness begins to fade.

"Be still and know
that I am God."

Embrace the stillness.

Discover God
in the
loneliness.

# ANGER

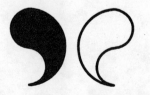

I got angry at a friend.

I hurt the feelings of
somebody that I love.

Now I am hurting and
my friend comforts me.

That's friendship.

Today I feel angry.

So!

Express your anger
today so that tomorrow
you can
smile.

Only when I accept the anger
that exists in me will I be free to
love myself and others.

Anger is not good or bad.

It is a feeling.

I see the pain in so many
people.  Millions starving ,
 lonely, afraid and weary.

I am angry.

Angry at God.
Angry at life.
Angry at myself.

Hopefully this anger will lead to
positive action!

I get angry at my
procrastination.

Always I am going to do
something … tomorrow.

But tomorrow needs to begin
today.

Anger.

Acceptance.

Two sides of the human coin.

The creative ingredients of life.

I saw anger on the face of a friend the other day.

It was a mirror into my own anger.

Now I see what I need to change.

Rage shouts and creates fear.

Rage is anger out of control.

Am I in rage?

No.

Because today there are
boundaries to my anger.

Does God get angry at our constant complaining?

Does God get angry at our apathy?

Does God … ?

We are made in the image of God.

Then God must get angry.

Only when
I am allowed
to express my
anger
am I truly loved.

# FEAR

Sometimes I just seem to fear
everything.

Fear the future, work, tomorrow,
relationships, God …

In confronting this fear, I
nourish trust and
self-confidence.

When I acknowledge my fears
I am able to understand
the fears of others.

The acceptance of fear
in all our lives
is the foundation
for real
relationships.

Those things that I most fear
have an uncanny way of
becoming reality.

Moral?

Don't give energy
to my fears.

I saw a man drunk,
unkempt, homeless and alone.

I was afraid.

What is the difference
between me and that man?

A beer.

Today I choose
not to take that first drink.

$\mathcal{S}$ometimes I fear the freedom
that God has entrusted to me.

I know that I can
create or destroy,
smile or frown,
befriend or hate.

Today
I respect
my fears.

God is perfect love.

Love is awesome.

Fear is
a mysterious
part of love.

Perhaps that is how
God is to be feared.

The fear
of being alone
energizes me
to seek
meaningful relationships.

We were not created
to be alone.

A man boasted that he had never been afraid.

I feel sorry for that man.

Fear is my bridge to other people.

Healthy relationships grow with the acknowledgement of my fears.

When I confront my fears I am on the road to conquering them.

Fear teaches me that I am not perfect.

Perfect love cast out fear.

Only God is perfect.

# ISOLATION

Sometimes I feel I am on the
outside of life looking in.

Then somebody smiles at me.

Now I am on the inside of life
looking for somebody
to smile at!

Today I have a choice:  I can
reach out or
remain isolated.

In the exercise of this
gift of choice
I can break my
imagined separation
from other people.

When I neglect the gift
of God's creativity
in my life
I experience isolation.

I belong in this world.

More importantly, the world
belongs to me.

Why do I isolate from people?

Because I am afraid of being
known.

But not to be known is isolation.

"Be still and  know
that I am God."

In those moments of utter
isolation God can be found.

Is it possible to be isolated from
God's love?

No.

The awareness of this miracle
enables creative living.

I cry:
"Nobody loves me!"

God says:
"Speak for yourself."

It's time
to get of
my pity-pot.

God created
everything
for me.
The kingdom
of God is
discovered
in the
awareness
of this truth.

God said,
"I am with you always."

Spirituality
is the knowledge
that complete isolation
is an illusion.

When I begin to talk about my feelings of isolation I discover that I am not alone.

# SHAME

I heard shaming messages from people who claimed to love me.

Then I realized that my beauty and specialness are not dependent on others.

Today I affirm:
I love myself.

Shame says:
"You are no good.

"You are ugly,
stupid and useless."

God proclaims:
"I don't make junk."

Shame destroys
my spiritual identity.

Spirituality always
requires me to nurture
self-acceptance
and
self-love.

Shaming comparisons
are the result
of ignorance.

Divinity
is experienced
in the acceptance
of my uniqueness.

Today I am not ashamed of
who I am.

This affirming acceptance frees
me to celebrate life.

Shame is the thief of
self-esteem.

Shame's weapon is comparison.

It denies our individuality.

Shame says: "How could you do such a thing?"

I reply: "Because today I understand that I am not perfect.

"But I am still loved by God."

$S$hame told me I was an unacceptable sinner.

Jesus exclaimed: "Let whoever is without sin cast the first stone."

Today I know that I am acceptable.

Shame creates fear.

When I confront
the fear,
I begin
the healing
of my shame.

$G$od created
the world
in delightful variety.

In our difference
God is perceived.

# JOY

I watched a child
build a sandcastle
on the beach
and I felt
a quiet joy.

Joy is
often experienced
in the simple
moments
of life.

We find joy
when we discover
the art of living
a grateful life.

Joy looked
at Depression
and said,
"You are sad
because you are blind
to the variety in life."

For those with
eyes to see,
life is a
continuous
miracle.

Amongst an avalanche
of depressing news
I read about a young man
who risked his life
to save a drowning kitten.

Joy comes with
knowing we are
creatures who can
selflessly care.

Last night a friend called
to say hello.

We talked about nothing.

Today, the memory of that
conversation is
something special.

Joy is in the ordinary.

God has invited us to help
create a better world.

This is our invitation to a divine
partnership.

Joy comes with knowing and
accepting this miracle.

God said, "Let there be love.

And let it include joy."

If we want to be happy, we must
discover in ourselves something
to love.

Then and only then
will we find joy.

$J$oy is
a process.

It is not
an event.

I experience joy
in understanding
that I do not
know everything.

Joy exists in the
awareness
of my imperfection.

Joy is knowledge.

Joy is love.

Joy is acceptance.

Always, joy is more
than any word
can express.

# ACCEPTANCE

God loves us.

This means that
we are accepted.

Even in our worst moments
God still loves us.

We cannot do anything
to separate ourselves
from God's love.

Spiritual acceptance involves
knowing that I am loved, and I
am capable of being a good
person.

Spirituality is knowing that I
have a responsibility for the life I
choose to live in this world.

Acceptance of God's love
involves an acceptance of
myself.

Once I am able to accept
my humanness,
then the burdens
of unrealistic
expectations
are removed.

Somebody I love
hurt me today
and I am sad.

Then I remember
the people I have hurt
over the years.

This allows me to accept
an overcome the hurt
from my friend.

Sometimes I want to use
alcohol, drugs, food, sex …
anything to escape my
confused and painful feelings.

But true acceptance
lets me see that
confusion and pain
are part of the process
of growth.

Acceptance
does not mean
that I have to like
what has happened.

"And the lion shall
lie down with the lamb."

Acceptance by the lion?

Surely.

Acceptance by the lamb?

Definitely.

I know
that God
has accepted me.

My struggle
is in
accepting
myself!

Love involves acceptance.

Forgiveness needs acceptance.

Growth requires acceptance.

Acceptance is the foundation of
healthy spirituality.

# LOVE

Sometimes
I confuse love
with security.

Love is
absorbing fear
into the joy of living.

Love is
feeling free enough
to express yourself
imperfectly.

Love is not about
ownership.

Sometimes
we need to love people enough
to let them go.

Hate says: "If you don't do what I ask, I will cease to love you."

Love says: "If you don't do what I ask, I will still accept you."

There are as many ways
to love
as there are people
to love.

Love reflects our diversity.

God loved us enough to risk
rejection. In the gift of our
spiritual freedom
God's creative love is
experienced.

"My love is like a
red, red rose."

But can I discover love
in loneliness,
fear and rejection?

Love requires the
acceptance of pain.

Love is discovering the beauty
in the beast.

Tough love is recognizing the
beast in the beauty.

"Do you love me?"

said the rabbit to the crocodile.

"Come close and I will show you," replied the crocodile.

Sometimes, love requires distance.

I find it hard to love some people.

At such times,
I "Let go and let God."

# FORGIVENESS

God's forgiveness
allows us the possibility
of making the same
mistake again.

Jesus said, "Father, forgive them, for they know not what they do."

Today I know what I have done.

And I know I am forgiven.

Now, I can forgive others.

In the act of forgiving others I experience forgiveness.

It is the awareness of human imperfection that creates the possibility of healthy relationships.

Forgiveness is a
neglected miracle.

In the gift of forgiveness we
experience joy, growth and
acceptance.

The disciple asked the teacher:
"Can you love without
forgiving?"

The teacher replied: "Can you
swim without water?"

Is it my fault
that I have
the possibility
of error?

The ability to forgive is a
precious gift.

Without forgiveness there could
be no relationships.

Without the ingredient
of forgiveness
we would suffocate
in controlled perfection.

Why do I find it so hard to forgive some people?

Because they reveal some aspects of me that I don't want to see.

Forgiveness requires rigorous honesty.

Today I need to forgive me.

When I can forgive myself
I know I am not God.

# SPIRITUALITY

Spirituality is discovering the
oneness of creation.

Spirituality unites that which
appears divided.

Religion
is man-made.

Spirituality
is God-given.

The spiritual life
is experienced
in being a positive
and creative human being.

The disciple asks: "Where can I find Spirituality?"

The teacher replies: "Spirituality is not a place.

"It must be discovered within the journey of your life."

$F$or those with
eyes to see,
everything that exists
pertains to Spirituality.

Spirituality has no barriers.

It brings together male and female, Jew and gentile, priest and atheist.

Spirituality is revealed in unity.

God
breathed life
into creation.

Spirituality records
our historical
"Yes!" to life.

$S$pirituality
accepts and rejoices
in the variety
of God's creation.

Spirituality reflects
the love that is
experienced
from God.

The disciple asked:
"Must you be good
to be spiritual?"

The teacher replied: "No.

"But you must be human."

About the Author...

Father

# LEO
# BOOTH

He's a different kind of priest who says you don't have to be religious to be spiritual. The dynamic Englishman is a spiritual 'rebel with a cause': He wants to bring spirituality back into religion, and help the essence of being real and human. An energetic mix of Charlie Chaplin with a touch of Dudley Moore, he's an Episcopal priest who's as likely to quote The Velveteen Rabbit as often as the Bible. He's not afraid to tweak the noses of religious and psychotherapy establishments to get his message across, but once he's heard, he treats his listeners with warmth, dignity, compassion and insight.

For over 17 years he has focused on helping people reclaim their spiritual power. A recovering alcoholic and certified addictions and eating disorders counselor, he is a national consultant to treatment programs and organizations. Rev. Booth is an active Episcopal priest in the Diocese of Los Angeles. He is the author of 6 books on the issues of spirituality and recovery.

# Books by Leo Booth

### THE ANGEL AND THE FROG

In this charming spiritual fable, Cedric the Frog and the residents of Olde Stable Farm meet an angel named Christine and discover the Spiritual Process.
*SCP Limited*

### THE GOD GAME — IT'S YOUR MOVE:
*Reclaim Your Spiritual Power*

We don't "get" spiritual. Our spirituality is built into us at creation, in the connection between Mental, Physical and Emotional. Claiming our spiritual power involves connecting to ourselves and learning to make our spiritually powerful moves.
*Stillpoint Publishing*

## WHEN GOD BECOMES A DRUG:
### *Breaking the Chains of*
### *Religious Addiction and Abuse*

This challenging and insightful look at the symptoms and sources of religious addiction and abuse is also a guide to attaining healthy spirituality.
*Putnam\Perigee*

## SAY YES TO LIFE: *Daily Meditations*

365 daily meditations on issues relating to alcoholism, chemical dependency, eating disorders and codependency.
*Scp Limited*

## MEDITATIONS FOR COMPULSIVE PEOPLE

In this collection of meditations in verse, Leo the poet meets Leo the theologian. Revised, with worksheet and process questions.
*Scp Limited*

## SPIRITUALITY AND RECOVERY

One of the most popular of Father Leo's works, this book is a guide to crating healthy spirituality in recovery. It explains the difference between religion and spirituality, and suggests ways in which to become a positive, creative person.
*SCP Limited*

# OTHER MATERIALS FROM LEO BOOTH

### 40 INDIVIDUAL AUDIOS
### and AUDIO ALBUMS ( 4 titles per set)

Individual audios and album sets on spirituality, religious abuse, self-empowerment, drug and alcohol abuse, codependency, relationship and life issues.

*VIDEOS*

An excellent addition to your recovery library, especially for treatment programs, hospitals, alcohol and drug councils. Each approximately 55 minutes running time.

V1 Say Yes To Life
V2 Meditations For Compulsive People
V3 Spirituality and Aduclt Children of Alcoholics Recovery
V4 Creating Healthy Relationships
V5 Recovery From An Eating Disorder
V6 Intervention: Creating an Opportunity to Live
V7 Overcoming Religious Addiction and Religious Abuse
V8 An Evening With Father Leo

## ANNUAL SPIRITUAL EMPOWERMENT CONFERENCE CRUISES AND RETREATS

Each year, Leo Booth presents conference cruises and retreats. During these fun-filled days, you'll explore all aspects of healthy spirituality, from the morning "Attitude of Gratitude" meeting to the evening dancing and play. Themes include manifesting your life's dreams, achieving goals, claiming spiritual power and healing spiritual wounds of addictions or other issues. Dates and itineraries vary from year to year. Space is limited and fills up quickly, so early reservations are recommended.

## CONFERENCES * WORKSHOPS * INSERVICES * CONSULTANCIES *

Leo Booth works with a variety of groups and organizations, from treatment centers and therapists, to the general public, teaching how to create healthy spirituality. The Spiritual Concepts staff will help you with any phase of the event, from choosing a topic to suggesting marketing strategies and creating ads and copy. If you would like to share his wit, wisdom and zest for life with your program or organization call Spiritual Concepts.

For a catalog and information call:

Spiritual Concepts
(800) 284-2804
(8:00 AM - 4:00 PM Pacific time Mon.- Fri.)
2700 St. Louis Avenue
Long Beach, CA 90806
Internet: www.fatherleo.com
E-Mail: frleo@deltanet.com